DINOSAURS
I HAVE KNOWN

by Barry Louis Polisar

Illustrations by Michael Stewart

ISBN No. 0-938663-00-3 hardback

DINOSAURS I HAVE KNOWN
by Barry Louis Polisar
© copyright 1986 by Barry Louis Polisar
All artwork © 1986 by Michael Stewart

Published by Rainbow Morning Music
2121 Fairland Road, Silver Spring, Md 20904

FIRST EDITION

Special thanks go to Sheldon Biber,
Nancy Heller and my wife, Roni,
who have helped in smoothing
out the rough spots and getting
me through the ice ages.

Table of Contents

Introduction

I have always been interested in dinosaurs. I have read about them and have searched for their fossils since childhood, finding a Hadrosaur tooth as far away as Alberta, Canada, and fossilized shark's teeth along the Chesapeake Bay.

In all my years of research and reading, I have been amazed to find that in almost every book and scholarly journal on dinosaurs I have read, paleontologists and other scientists seem to dwell exclusively on the most popular dinosaurs. Little, if anything, is ever written on other, lesser-known dinosaurs. And nowhere do books tell what dinosaurs were *really* like.

We now know that dinosaurs had problems just like everyone else. They sat in rush-hour traffic and couldn't get good service in restaurants. There were dinosaurs employed as plumbers (somebody had to fix the pipes back then), and dinosaurs who worked as doctors, lawyers and telephone operators. This book, hopefully, will provide an introduction—and insight—into the everyday lives of some of those dinosaurs—long gone, and otherwise forgotten.

Barry Louis Polisar
Spring 1986

Surfosaurus

(pronounced Surf-oh-sore-us)

The Surfosaurus was a fun-loving dinosaur, believed to have lived in what is now Southern California. Known for its long legs and dark, sun-tanned complexion, this agile little creature was a plant-eater. Paleontologists believe it spent many hours in the Pacific, riding the waves—until the big one hit. Frequently seen wearing sandals and Hawaiian shirts, the Surfosaurus was usually surrounded by adoring admirers. It loved anything to do with water and existed primarily by drinking liquids of all kinds.

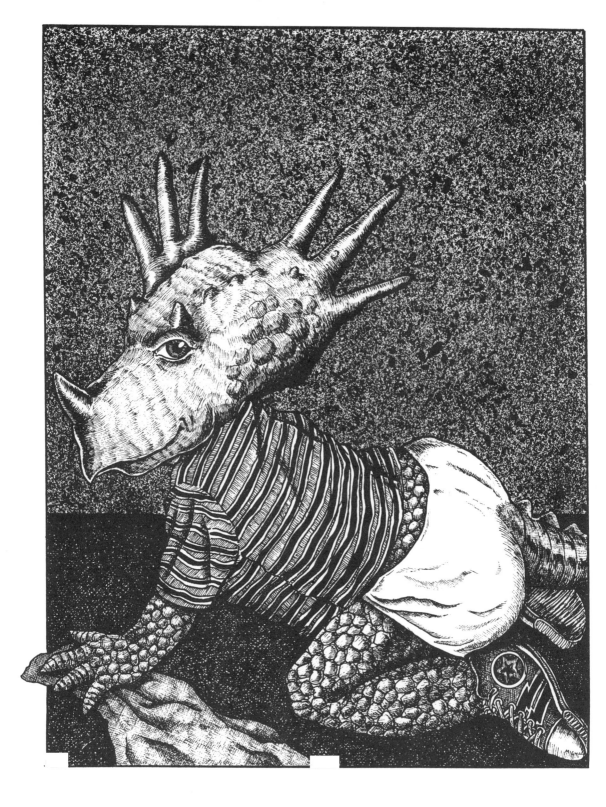

Diaperashopus
(pronounced Dye-per-rash-oh-pus)

This dinosaur had many problems. It was continually being teased by other dinosaurs, which made it very self-conscious. Always clad in a diaper, the Diaperashopus traveled slowly and perpetually had a very bad rash on its rear. A large dinosaur, the Diaperashopus was a funny sight; it generally waddled like a duck and was frequently seen carrying a teddy bear and bottle...not a mature dinosaur.

Snifflesaurus

(pronounced Sniff-el-saw-russ)

Related to the Staphylococcus Rex, the Snifflesaurus was perhaps best known for its ability to catch colds, which, it is theorized, led to its ultimate extinction. Like a Brontosaurus with bronchitis, the Snifflesaurus had a high body temperature and spent much of its time taking vitamins and drinking orange juice. Even this could not put off its colds—or its eventual demise. Always polite, this dinosaur did what it was told and never talked back to anyone, even when told to go outside and play in the tar pits.

Chasidic Chadrosaur
(pronounced Ha-sid-ik Had-ro-sawr)

Recent research has indicated that this dinosaur wore dark clothing and loved to dance in circles. A happy dinosaur, the male Chasidic Chadrosaur had a long beard and curly locks and would frequently wave his arms in the air to make a point. Believed to be related to the Tsoorisaurus, the Chasidic Chadrosaurs were very religious and were often seen in prayer. Their favorite foods included herring and other smoked fish and their meals were almost always festive occasions for family gatherings. The discovery of the Chasidic Chadrosaur suggests that there was a great deal of ethnic and cultural diversity among dinosaurs.

Saxosaurus
(pronounced Sax-oh-saw-russ)

One of many urban dinosaurs, the Saxosaurus was most often found in the inner city. It slept during the day and was active nocturnally. A love of music characterized the Saxosaurus and it would often entertain neighboring dinosaurs with its piercing, soulful melodies. Frequently found in nightclubs and coffeehouses, the Saxosauri developed a subculture of their own, including a specialized dialect and vocabulary. Favorite expressions included "I'm hip," "Dig it," and "Man," the last being a reference to an early Cro-Magnon species that ran the local grocery store. The Saxosaurus was known to have associated with saber-toothed cats. It is believed that inhaling secondhand smoke led to its extinction.

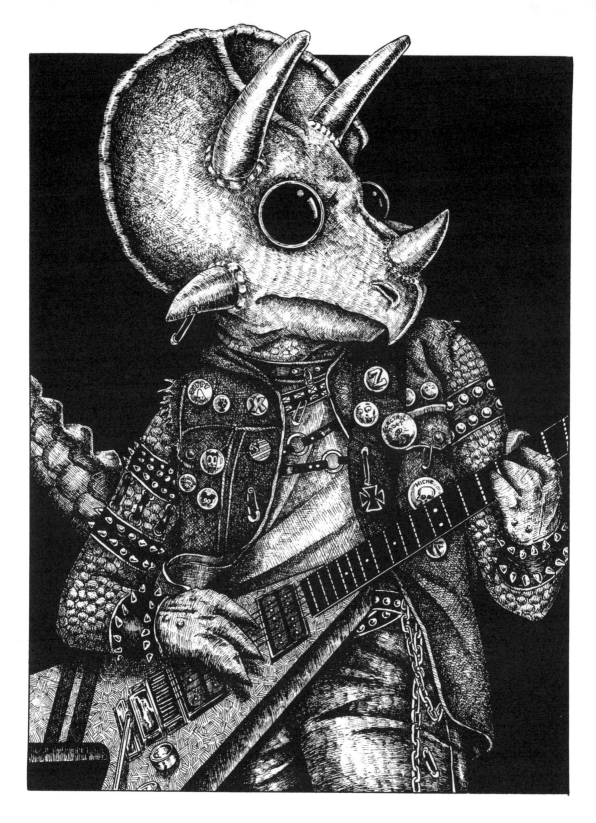

Punkaceratops

(pronounced Punk-ah-cer-a-tops)

Known for its outlandish dress and spiked hairdos, the Punkaceratops existed during the Cacophonic era. Its body and limbs were protected by plates and spikes and an array of buttons covered its torso. Its long tail acted to balance its considerable weight. It loved loud music and discordant rhythms and was known to paint its scales in bright, clashing colors. The Punkaceratops was generally seen in urban areas, but loved to go to suburban shopping malls where it would frequently frighten other dinosaurs with its outrageous outfits. Despite its appearance and behavior, however, there is no indication that the Punkaceratops was a flesh eater.

Touristsaurus

(Pronounced Tour-ist-saw-russ)

The Touristsauri were an abused group, preyed upon by almost every meat-eating dinosaur. They ate poorly and their ability to camouflage themselves was virtually nonexistent. They were easily recognized by the way they dressed and acted and their long, extended necks seemed perfectly fitted for the cameras they were often seen carrying. As nomadic dinosaurs, they traveled frequently and rarely stayed long in any one place. They were often accompanied by their children, who cried and complained constantly. Fossilized callus patterns discovered in a hardened river-bed near the Grand Canyon have led paleontologists to theorize that the Touristsauri stood on their hind legs for long hours.

Rockadopolis Rex

(pronounced Rock-a-dop-a-lis Rex)

Also known as "The King," the Rockadopolis Rex is believed to have existed in the Sporadic era. It had a long waist which it would shake vigorously, attracting other dinosaurs who would flock around it, screaming and shouting. It played the guitar and in its early years was featured in many badly-made movies. In spite of this, pictures of this dinosaur embossed on plates and coffee mugs have been found in many prehistoric excavation sites. Its favorite hobbies included eating. An overly indulgent dinosaur, the Rockadopolis Rex is believed to have self-destructed.

Orthodontosaurus

(Pronounced Orth-oh-don-ta-saw-russ)

A very rich reptilian, the Orthodontosaurus was known for its perfect bite. Little else is known about this dinosaur except that it was a small, lightly-built reptile, with a flat head and a very large bill. It was also known as Braciosaurus (pronounced Brace-ee-oh-sore-us). Due to infrequent brushing and an improper diet, almost all dinosaurs had tooth problems requiring the services of the Orthodontosaurus. Thanks to their work, many perfect dental specimens have been preserved for study.

Cosmopolitanathus
(pronounced Cos-mo-pol-it-an-uh-thus)

A highly sophisticated dinosaur known for its fondness for fancy restauraunts and overpriced clothing, the Cosmopolitanathus was both fashionable and socially correct. It roamed the country looking for designer clothes and elegant parties. Though not a predator itself, the Cosmopolitanathus frequently fed on other dinosaurs, such as the Oniondiplodocus, which was often served at chic dinosaur parties. A fan of old Fred Astaire and Ginger Rogers movies, the Cosmopolitanathus loved to dance and was often seen at lavish affairs.

The Brontësaurus Sisters

(pronounced Bron-tay-saw-russ Sis-ters)

The Brontësaurus Sisters (Emily, Charlotte and Anne) were early Victorian dinosaurs known for their literary genius. Among the most educated of all dinosaurs, they lived in the Prosaic era. Recently discovered bones support the theory that they were lightly-built, two-legged, meat-eating dinosaurs. Some scientists have theorized that they wore plumes on the backs of their heads and were related to the stately Thesaurus Rex. They were well-dressed and well-behaved, as was suitable for the times in which they lived. They drank tea, ate their meals in small portions, and spent long hours in their rooms, hovering over their typewriters trying to finish their manuscripts. Psychologists now believe that severe depression and sibling rivalry were the main factors that led to their demise, each trying to write more–and better–than her sisters.

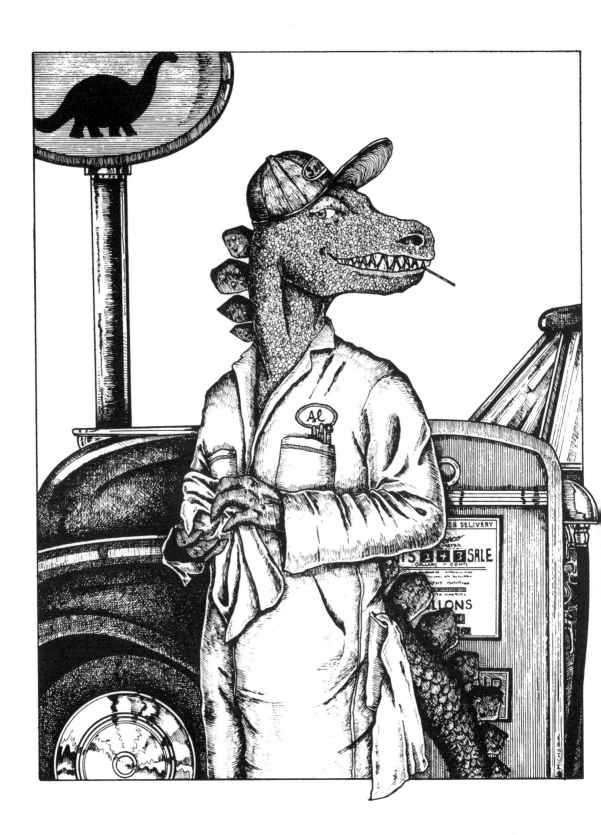

Sinclairosaurus
(pronounced Sin-clare-oh-saw-russ)

The Sinclairosaurus was the last known dinosaur to become extinct. It thrived well into the 1960's in an otherwise modern age. It prospered until a change in climate caused conditions to shift, spurring development of larger, more adept species which the Sinclairosaurus could not fight off. It was devoured by the Conglomeratosaurus, which successfully adapted to change by swallowing smaller creatures. The Conglomeratosaurus has camouflaged its dinosaur ancestry, but not its desire to consume others. Now it's Beatrice.

Gluttonous Rex

(pronounced Glut-ton-us Rex)

The Gluttonous Rex had grasping hands and large eyes and was a predatory dinosaur. It killed its prey and tore it to pieces, which it then sold to other dinosaurs at a profit. Related to the Piranhasaurus, it was a very fat, overweight dinosaur, frequently protected by the Lawyersaurus (a dinosaur of the Oratorius Rex family that was done in by inbreeding and overpopulation). It frequently wore gold chains around its neck and large rings on its fingers and was responsible for making many decisions that affected thousands of other dinosaurs. It frequently worked as a record merchandiser or television producer.

Sauroritoidees

(Saur-or-uh-toy-dees)

Predecessors of the modern-day sorority sisters found on many college campuses, the Sauroritoidees lived on a diet of French fries and hamburgers, which scientists feel contributed to their early demise. They traveled in small groups and usually searched for their food at night. They were strongly influenced by popular culture and tried not to think for themselves. Favorite pastimes included whatever was popular at the moment. They loved to wander aimlessly through shopping malls, go to movies, and listen to the radio while driving in their cars. When together, they would talk about Fratrosaurs and giggle frequently. Mature Sauroritoidees were much more reserved—some became petrified while still living.

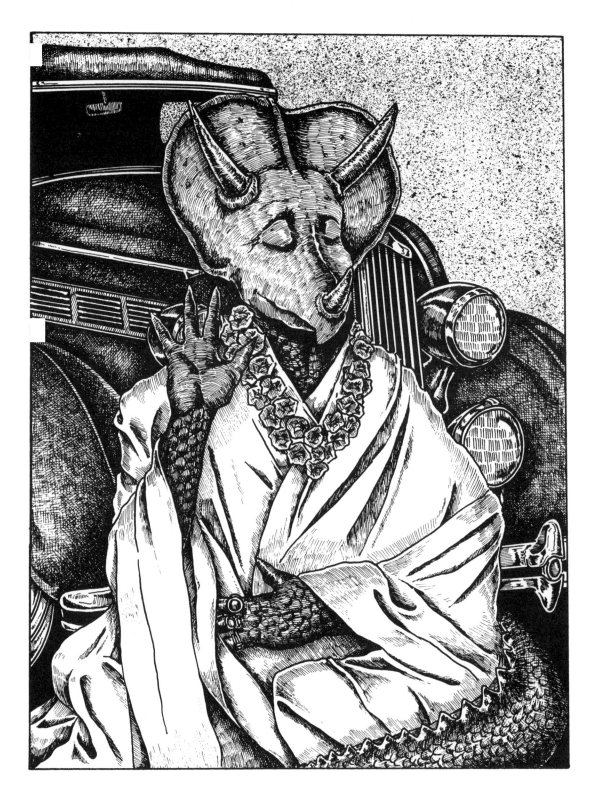

Triswamitops

(pronounced Try-swa-mee-tops)

The Triswamitops was a meditative dinosaur which attracted thousands of disciples. It preached a quiet, spiritual life but when its bones were discovered they had been gold-plated. The Triswamitops owned many automobiles, as well as four jets and a string of fast-food restaurants. It spoke infrequently and made small grunting sounds which were interpreted by its followers as a mantra or meditative chant. We know this dinosaur had many devotees because of the number of bones found beside it. It is theorized that the Triswamitops ate its followers.

Stagasaurus
(pronounced Stag-ah-saw-russ)

The Stagasaurus was one of the last dinosaurs to become extinct. These "stags," as they liked to call themselves, were a group of dinosaurs who hung out in clubs that did not permit female members. Their short necks and thick skulls were covered with horny lumps and knobs that grew larger as they aged. They would gather together to drink, smoke, and play golf.

Voluptuous Rex

(pronounced Vo-lup-chew-us Rex)

A typical show-biz dinosaur, it was originally believed this creature had a large build and a very small brain. In later years, just prior to its extinction, the Voluptuous Rex entertained other dinosaurs with its songs of love and betrayal and was frequently found in the company of playwrights and politicians. Paleontologists now believe that this dinosaur was much more advanced than had previously been thought and its life has recently been the subject of numerous books by noted authors.

Struthiomime

(pronounced Strooth-ee-oh-mime)

This dinosaur was fond of imitating others. Dating from the Esoteric era, the Struthiomime walked on its hind legs and had a long neck and pointy head. Its long tail helped it to balance itself, which it did very well. The Struthiomime was frequently found on city streets wearing silly hats and frilly costumes. It seldom spoke. It was often seen at shopping malls and festivals juggling brightly-colored objects and trying to attract attention. Unfortunately, the Struthiomime was ignored by most other dinosaurs. When other dinosaurs became extinct, it imitated them.

Dinosaur Provincial Park

Certified Fossil Finder

The honor of Certified Fossil Finder is hereby awarded to _____Barry Louis Polisar_____ on this ____30th____ day of _____July_____ , ___1982___ to acknowledge reporting a significant fossil discovery in Dinosaur Provincial Park which contributes to the park's scientific and paleontological record.

_____
Minister

_____
Issuing Officer

Alberta
RECREATION AND PARKS

Duck-billed Dinosaur

In addition to having discovered the tooth of a Hadrosaur in Alberta, Canada, Barry Louis Polisar is a children's poet and songwriter. He has published over 100 songs and poems (including a few about dinosaurs) and has recorded seven albums and cassettes of his songs. He has published a volume of poetry, songs and drawings for children, entitled NOISES FROM UNDER THE RUG as well as DON'T DO THAT! A CHILD'S GUIDE TO BAD MANNERS, RIDICULOUS RULES AND INADEQUATE ETIQUETTE. He is currently working on a number of books for children, including THE HAUNTED HOUSE PARTY, a story in poetry form about a Halloween party that gets taken over by real ghosts and goblins. Barry travels all over the United States and Canada giving concerts in schools, libraries and art centers. He is married and lives in Silver Spring, Maryland.

In addition to working as an artist and illustrator, Michael Stewart is a third-generation photographer and dinosaur hunter. He has collaborated with Barry on NOISES FROM UNDER THE RUG as well as many other projects. He is not married and lives in Silver Spring, Maryland.